Flip the Flaps
Seashore

Hannah Wilson and Simon Mendez

KINGFISHER
NEW YORK

KINGFISHER
LONDON & NEW YORK

Copyright © Kingfisher 2010
Published in the United States by Kingfisher,
175 Fifth Ave., New York, NY 10010
Kingfisher is an imprint of Macmillan Children's Books, London.
All rights reserved.

Distributed in the U.S. and Canada by Macmillan,
175 Fifth Ave., New York, NY 10010

Consultant: David Burnie

First published in hardback by Kingfisher in 2010
First published in paperback by Kingfisher in 2012

Library of Congress Cataloging-in-Publication data has been applied for.

ISBN: 978-0-7534-6951-4

Kingfisher books are available for special promotions and premiums. For details contact:
Special Markets Department, Macmillan, 175 Fifth Ave., New York, NY 10010.

For more information, please visit www.kingfisherbooks.com

Printed in China
1 3 5 7 9 8 6 4 2
1TR/0912/UTD/LFA/157GEMA

Contents

In the rock pool

Many creatures live in
rock pools along the seashore.
When the tide is out, there
might not be much water
inside the pool. When the
tide is in, the rock pool fills
up and bright anemones
uncurl their tentacles.

shell

rock pool at
low tide

starfish

4

1. A hermit crab lives inside the empty shell of a sea snail. The hard shell protects the crab's soft body.

2. The anemone sticks out its poisonous tentacles, which sting tiny sea creatures and push them toward its mouth.

3. Limpets, barnacles, and mussels grow shells and attach themselves to rocks.

anemone's tentacles

Creatures that cling to rocks

limpets

barnacles

mussels

5

On the salt marsh

When the sea floods the land, salty marshes can form. Thick with rushes and reeds, they are home to many different birds, including flamingos.

flamingo chick

1. A flamingo stands on one leg to keep warm and dry and to rest.

2. Flamingos are pink because they eat so many pink shrimp!

3. In addition to birds, insects and snakes hide among the watery plants of salt marshes.

Other animals on the salt marsh

green-winged teal

dragonfly

Gulf water snake

7

Snowy seashores

In the coldest parts of the world, animals live by the sea to hunt for food in its icy waters. Thick layers of fat, fur, or feathers keep the animals warm.

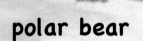

polar bear

male walrus (a bull)

mother walrus and her pup

1. A polar bear lives on the ice so that it can hunt seals for food.

2. Walrus have tusks and whiskers. A female walrus has shorter tusks than a male walrus. A baby walrus has no tusks at all.

3. Some penguins slide down icy slopes on their stomachs to splash into the sea.

Penguins like to . . .

waddle,

slide on their stomachs,

and dive into the water!

9

On the beach

When a wave washes up on the beach, it drops shells and seaweed onto the sand. The wave also leaves behind tiny creatures for crabs and wading birds to eat.

hungry seagulls

sandcastle

"mermaid's purse" (egg case)

crab

hidden starfish

10

1. Crabs are difficult to catch because they have hard shells. They also move sideways, which confuses birds.

2. A starfish usually has five legs. If a crab or fish eats one leg, the starfish may grow another!

3. Pretty seashells and clumps of slimy seaweed wash up on the beach. If you see a jellyfish, don't touch it—it can sting!

Things found on the beach

shells

seaweed

jellyfish

11

Salty swamps

In hot parts of the world, salty swamps called mangrove swamps meet the sea. Filled with plants and trees, they are home to fish, frogs, crabs, and furry animals such as monkeys and otters.

fishing cat

long-tailed macaque monkeys

1. Some monkeys swim in the sea to cool down or to hunt fish and crabs for dinner.

2. The fishing cat taps the water with its paw, pretending to be an insect. When a fish comes to investigate, the cat scoops it out.

3. The mother and father otters dig a burrow near the water. The babies are born inside the burrow.

Taking care of baby otters

mother and father otters

otter pups outside burrow

learning to swim

13

Rocky islands

Many seashore animals live
on islands far out at sea.
They have their babies on
land, among the rocks and
cliffs, but dive deep into
the ocean to find food.

iguanas
sunbathing

14

1. Marine iguanas dive into the cold sea to eat sea plants. They sunbathe on rocks to warm up again.

2. Some male marine iguanas turn pink to attract females. All the lizards spray sea salt out of their noses. This makes their faces white!

3. Puffins make nests by digging burrows on a grassy cliff top.

How puffins live on cliffs

mother and baby chick

inside a burrow

diving for fish

Nighttime on the beach

The seashore can be safer for some animals at night. Predators (animals that hunt other animals) find it hard to hunt in the darkness. Bats, however, are excellent nighttime hunters.

loggerhead turtle

1. A turtle likes to lay her eggs in a sandy burrow on a beach.

2. The turtle lays about 100 eggs. They look like Ping-Pong balls!

laying eggs

3. A fisherman bat (or bulldog bat) hunts at night. It flies along the beach and catches fish with its feet.

How a fisherman bat hunts

swooping across water

snatching up a fish

flying away

17

Index

1. Who lives inside a shell?

2. How does an anemone catch its dinner?

3. Which creatures cling to rocks?

closed
anemone

hermit crab living
inside shell

blenny

submerged
rock pool

1. How does a flamingo keep warm?

2. Why are flamingos pink?

3. Which animals live in salt marshes?

standing
on one leg

eating tiny
shrimp

1. Why does a polar bear live on the ice?

2. Which animals have tusks like an elephant and whiskers like a cat?

3. How do penguins splash into the sea?

catching
a seal

walrus pup wakes up

1. Why are crabs difficult for seagulls to catch?

2. How many legs does a starfish have?

3. What can you find on the beach?

1. Do monkeys swim in the sea?

2. How does a fishing cat catch fish?

3. How do smooth-coated otters take care of their babies?

jumping

splashing around

1. Which lizards live
by the sea?

2. Why are some marine
iguanas pink and white?

3. Where do puffins make
their nests?

spraying
salt

1. Why does a turtle
like the beach?

2. How many eggs does
a loggerhead turtle lay?

3. Which "fisherman"
hunts at night?